CAMBRIDGE LIBRARY COLLECTION

Books of enduring scholarly value

Religion

For centuries, scripture and theology were the focus of prodigious amounts of scholarship and publishing, dominated in the English-speaking world by the work of Protestant Christians. Enlightenment philosophy and science, anthropology, ethnology and the colonial experience all brought new perspectives, lively debates and heated controversies to the study of religion and its role in the world, many of which continue to this day. This series explores the editing and interpretation of religious texts, the history of religious ideas and institutions, and not least the encounter between religion and science.

A Doubter's Doubts About Science and Religion

This 1889 volume was published anonymously and later ascribed to Robert Anderson, a barrister and theological writer who became Assistant Commissioner at Scotland Yard. Mixing his religious beliefs with his detective skills, Anderson argues for true scepticism to be embraced, comparing the tricks played on people by organised religion and science to the scams of confidence tricksters. Writing from a self-confessed standpoint of 'destructive criticism', Anderson discredits the theory of evolution as a newfangled superstition. Science, he says, assumes the existence of life, but has not the answer to the basic question – how did man come to be? 'The man who can give no account of his existence is a fool, and he who denies a god can give no account of his existence.' A Doubter's Doubts About Science and Religion proposes that the true sceptic cannot deny that the origin of life exists under the name of 'God'.

Cambridge University Press has long been a pioneer in the reissuing of out-of-print titles from its own backlist, producing digital reprints of books that are still sought after by scholars and students but could not be reprinted economically using traditional technology. The Cambridge Library Collection extends this activity to a wider range of books which are still of importance to researchers and professionals, either for the source material they contain, or as landmarks in the history of their academic discipline.

Drawing from the world-renowned collections in the Cambridge University Library, and guided by the advice of experts in each subject area, Cambridge University Press is using state-of-the-art scanning machines in its own Printing House to capture the content of each book selected for inclusion. The files are processed to give a consistently clear, crisp image, and the books finished to the high quality standard for which the Press is recognised around the world. The latest print-on-demand technology ensures that the books will remain available indefinitely, and that orders for single or multiple copies can quickly be supplied.

The Cambridge Library Collection will bring back to life books of enduring scholarly value across a wide range of disciplines in the humanities and social sciences and in science and technology.

A Doubter's Doubts About Science and Religion

By a Criminal Lawyer

ROBERT ANDERSON

CAMBRIDGE
UNIVERSITY PRESS

CAMBRIDGE UNIVERSITY PRESS

Cambridge New York Melbourne Madrid Cape Town Singapore São Paolo Delhi

Published in the United States of America by Cambridge University Press, New York

www.cambridge.org
Information on this title: www.cambridge.org/9781108000147

© in this compilation Cambridge University Press 2009

This edition first published 1889
This digitally printed version 2009

ISBN 978-1-108-00014-7

A DOUBTER'S DOUBTS

ABOUT SCIENCE AND RELIGION

A

DOUBTER'S DOUBTS

ABOUT SCIENCE AND RELIGION

BY

A CRIMINAL LAWYER

LONDON

KEGAN PAUL, TRENCH & CO., 1, PATERNOSTER SQUARE

1889

INTRODUCTORY NOTE.

THIS book needs no preface. The preface is too often used as a literary *hold-all*—that nondescript addition to the legitimate *impedimenta* of a journey, into which are stowed away all sorts of things which should have found room in the portmanteaus. It ought, however, to be strictly limited to matter personal to the author, or needed as a preliminary explanation of his "argument." But no one who will be at the pains to peruse these pages need have any doubt as to their purpose and aim, and the writer's anonymity ousts the personal element altogether.

A DOUBTER'S DOUBTS

ABOUT SCIENCE AND RELIGION.

———◆◇◆———

CHAPTER I.

"ONE of the first and noblest of human sciences "—such is the eulogy which Edmund Burke has pronounced upon the law. "It is," he goes on to say, "a science which does more to quicken and invigorate the understanding than all other kinds of learning put together." And if this estimate be just, it will probably be admitted that, for sharpening the intellect, the study and practice of the criminal law must bear the palm. But moral qualities are of greater worth than mere

B

quick-wittedness, and no one who has much
to do with criminals and crime can fail to
suffer morally. We are told that the primitive attitude of the human mind is trust;
distrust is the prevailing characteristic of any
one who sees much of the shady side of
human nature. He degenerates into a sort
of high-class detective. By a perverted
instinct he becomes systematically sceptical.

There are no sceptics in the old scholastic
sense. The most ardent Pyrrhonist, if
robbed of his purse, or struck over the head
by a burglar, promptly forgets his theories,
and gives proof of his belief in the certainty
of objective knowledge. Philosophic scepticism, so called, is merely a conceit of sham
philosophers; it never invades the sphere in
which a man's interests require that he should
believe and know. And, as Kant has aptly
said, it is "not a permanent resting-place for
human reason." But scepticism is not necessarily Pyrrhonism. Pyrrho did not invent

the word ; he only perverted and degraded it. The σκεπτικός considers, reflects, hesitates, doubts.   An admirable habit, surely, if kept within due limits, but proof of moral deterioration if abnormally developed.

And no one is so sensible of this kind of deterioration as the man who himself has suffered it.   He almost envies the ingenuousness of folk who accept a banknote without looking at the water-mark, and never ring a coin upon the counter.   And yet these very people value his judgment and advice when they find themselves in a difficulty ; and his power to help them largely depends upon his habit of reflecting, hesitating, doubting.   May not this habit of mind, then, be turned to account for the help of others, in higher and more important matters than fee-marked briefs ever deal with ?

We have all heard of "the confidence trick." With unfailing certainty it comes up again and again in our police reports, and we always read the story with mingled feelings of wonder, amusement, and pity. Nor is it merely the rustic and the tourist in the streets of London who fall victims to such frauds. By an artifice quite as silly and transparent one of our greatest city houses was not long since defrauded of £20,000 in gold. The details of the swindle would be delightful reading, but to divulge them would involve a breach of faith, for the merchants preferred to bear their loss, rather than incur the ridicule which publicity would have brought on them. But there are developments and phases of the "confidence trick" of which the police court takes no cognizance, and where the victim's loss cannot be estimated at a money value. Simple folk are every day imposed upon by deceptions just as shameless, palmed off upon them in the name of religion. And not of religion only, but of science also. And may not a sceptic do good service here? Is this not work for a high-class detective? It cannot be, surely, but that some at least will be found to appreciate an honest effort to expose such frauds.

CHAPTER II.

THERE is one fact which not even the dreamiest of egoists can doubt, and that is, his own existence. Here at least knowledge is absolute. I exist: this is certain. But how did I come to exist? I live: how did life begin? The question is one to which every man is bound to find a reasonable answer. To say I am descended through generations numbered or innumerable from a first man, is merely to put the difficulty back. Where did the first man come from? Religion answers in one word — Creation. But this is to cut the knot, as it were, without even an attempt to untie it. It must not be taken for granted that man is incapable of reasoning out the problem of his own existence.

Between the higher organisms and the lowest there is a gulf which might well be regarded as impassable. But closer observation and fuller knowledge will disclose the fact that between these extremes there are unnumbered gradations of development, and that the distance between the several steps in the series is such as might be passed by the operation of known laws. The problem, therefore, which religion would solve by the one word "creation," science answers by the one word "evolution." And science claims priority of audience.

But, as we proceed, let us not forget to reflect, hesitate, doubt; and, above all, let us cast away prejudice. Let us take the place of free thinkers and *real* sceptics, not shams. Many people reserve their scepticism for the sphere in which religion is the teacher, while in the presence of science they are as innocent and simple in their receptivity as the infant class in a Sunday-school. We shall only deceive ourselves if we begin by over-stating the evidence on which the doctrine of evolution rests. It must be conceded that its foundation largely depends on the researches of the Paleontologist. And here we demand some direct proof that the fossil remains belong to the same economy or system as the living organisms we compare them with. But there is no such proof, and it is a question whether the presumption be not the other way.

Let that pass, however, for a more serious question claims attention. It may be admitted that the development of plants and animals from their simplest to their most complicated forms may be explained by natural causes. But this is only theory. What direct evidence is there that the phenomena have, in fact, been thus produced? The horse may have been developed from a pig-like animal, and man may be "descended from a hairy quadruped furnished with a tail and pointed ears." * But what direct proof is there that either the horse or the man was, in fact, developed or evolved in this way? The answer must be, Absolutely none. It is a matter of inference only.†

The prisoner in the dock may have committed the murder we are investigating. The theory of his guilt will account for all the facts. Therefore let him be convicted and hanged. This sort of argument would not pass at the Old Bailey. Men are sceptics there, and free thinkers. Proof that the prisoner may have committed the crime is worthless, unless we go on to prove that it could not have been committed by any one else. But with that further proof the case is clear, and the accused goes to the gallows. And so here. If the facts of biology can in

* *Descent of Man*, pt. ii. chap. xxi.

† Marvellous results are produced by culture, but they are subject to the seemingly inexorable laws of degeneracy and the sterility of hybrids.

no other way be accounted for, evolution holds the field.

But are we not forgetting the nature of the problem to be solved? The first and greatest question relates, not to the phenomena of life, but to its origin. How did life begin? That was the question we set out with. And here evolution affords no answer, and must stand aside. Let the existence of life be taken for granted, and evolution will explain the rest. But the sceptic takes nothing for granted. How did life begin? Science answers ———! In presence of a question which lies across the threshold of knowledge, science, the very impersonification of knowledge, turns agnostic and is dumb. "Creation" is the answer religion gives. The rejoinder which science ought to make is that life first sprang out of death, out of nothing; in a word, abiogenesis.

And this is, in fact, the answer which science would formerly have given. But the experiments which at one time seemed to establish the principle of spontaneous generation, have proved worthless when subjected to severer tests. Professor Huxley admits that "the present state of knowledge furnishes us with no link between the living and the not living." With still greater candour, Professor Tyndall declares that "every attempt made in our day to generate life independently of antecedent life has utterly broken down." Or, if we turn to a teacher whose *dictum* will carry still greater weight, Sir William Thomson will tell us that "inanimate matter cannot become living except under the influence of matter already living. This is a fact in science which seems to me (he declares), as well ascertained as the law of gravitation." And he goes on to say, "I am ready to accept as an article of faith in science, valid for all time and in all space, that life is produced by life, and only by life." *

* Brit. Assoc., Edinburgh, 1871.

Abiogenesis is a mere philosophic theory, unsupported by even the faintest shadow of evidence. But more than this, it is practically incapable of proof, for the problem implies the proof of a negative in circumstances which render the difficulties of such proof overwhelming. To establish the fact of spontaneous generation in a world teeming with life, would be as hopeless as the attempt to prove that the displacement of a table in a dark room crowded with people was caused without interference on their part.*

But, we are told, the fact that we know absolutely nothing of the origin of life, and that there is not a shadow of direct evidence that abiogenesis has ever taken place, does not interfere with the conclusion "that at some time or other abiogenesis *must* have taken place. If the hypothesis of evolution be

---

* And if the proof were given, it would be more reasonable, more philosophical, to assume the presence of some unseen agency—*i.e.*, to fall back upon spiritualism—than to suppose the furniture capable of spontaneous motion.

true, living matter must have arisen from not-living matter." * Therefore life did originate thus, and the truth of evolution is established. Thus argue the professors and scientists. But the man who considers, reflects, hesitates, doubts, will call for the evidence ; and, finding there is none, he will reject the conclusion, and also, if necessary, the dependent hypothesis.

We set out to solve the mystery of life. Science claimed to possess the clew, and offered to be our guide. And now, having been led back to the identical point from which we started, we are told we must shut our eyes and take a leap in the dark. It is a bad case of the " confidence trick."

" Besides being absolutely without evidence to give it external support, this hypothesis cannot support itself internally—cannot be framed into a coherent thought. It is one of those illegitimate symbolic conceptions so

* Professor Huxley, *Encyc. Brit.*, " Biology."

continually mistaken for legitimate symbolic conceptions, because they remain untested. Immediately an attempt is made to elaborate the idea into anything like a definite shape, it proves to be a pseud-idea, admitting of no definite shape." It "implies the establishment of a relation in thought between nothing and something—a relation of which one term is absent—an impossible relation." " The case is one of those where men do not really believe, but rather *believe* they believe. For belief, properly so called, implies a mental representation of the thing believed ; and no such mental representation is here possible." *

Evolution assumes the existence of life ; postulates it, as the scientists would say. No more is needed than one solitary germ of living matter. Indeed, to seek for more would

* The words are **Mr.** Herbert Spencer's (*Principles of Biology*, § 112), the application of them is entirely my own.

be unphilosophical.* But this primeval germ must be taken for granted. The sceptic will refuse to assign to it an origin which contradicts all our experience and surpasses our knowledge. The only hypothesis he can accept is that life has existed without any limitation of time ; that the original life-germ was eternal and practically self-existent.

And of course nothing could be evolved from it which was not inherent. It must have been pregnant with all the forms and developments of life with which the world is full. Moreover it is only ignorant conceit to maintain that evolution has reached its limits. If man has sprung from such an origin, we must suppose that, in the far-distant future, beings

---

* " If all living beings have been evolved from pre-existing forms of life, it is enough that a single particle of living protoplasm should have once appeared on the globe, as the result of no matter what agency. In the eyes of a consistent evolutionist any further independent formation of protoplasm would be sheer waste."—Professor Huxley, *Encyc. Brit.*, " Biology."

will be developed as superior to mankind as we ourselves are superior to the insects crawling on the earth. According to the hypothesis the latent capacities of the first life-germ were infinite. " Capacities," remember, not tendencies. Unknowable force may account for tendencies, but it cannot create capacities.

Not that this distinction will save us from the pillory. The philosopher will condemn the statement as unphilosophical—" a shaping of ignorance into the semblance of knowledge " and I know not what besides.* But

* *Principles of Biology*, § 144. I have no wish to shelter myself behind Professor Huxley, but I claim his companionship and sympathy in the pillory. He says, " Of the causes which have led to the origination of living matter, then, it may be said that we know absolutely nothing. But postulating the existence of living matter endowed with that power of hereditary transmission and with that tendency to vary which is found in all such matter, Mr. Darwin has shown good reasons for believing," etc. (*Encyc. Brit.*, " Biology "). The primordial germ, mark, is " endowed " with a " power " and a " tendency." What has Mr. Spencer to say to this? All that I assert here is the " power ; " to predicate the " tendency " is unnecessary and therefore unphilosophical.

these brave words can be tested at once by assuming the contrary to what is here asserted. Let us take it, then, that the primordial germ had no latent capacities whatever. And yet we are to accept it as the origin of all the amazing forms and phenomena of life in the world. If we may not suppose such an aptitude naturally possessed by organisms, we must assume an *in*aptitude ; and the question is no longer whether the cause be adequate to the effects, but whether effects are to be ascribed to what is no cause at all. May we not retort that this is indeed "a cause unrepresentable in thought"—one of those illegitimate symbolic conceptions which cannot by any mental process be elaborated into a real conception ? *
In the spirit of a true philosopher, Charles Darwin will tell us that "the birth both of the species and of the individual are equally parts of that grand sequence of events which

* *Principles of Biology,* § 144.

C

our minds refuse to accept as the result of blind chance."*

By what word, then, shall this "particle of living protoplasm" be called ; this great First Cause ; this Life-germ, eternal, self-existent, infinite in essential capacities? There is but one word known to human language adequate to designate it, and that word is GOD.

Evolution—that is, Science—thus leads us to a point at which either we must blindly and with inexpressible credulity accept as fact something which is not only destitute of proof, but which is positively disproved by every test we are at present able to apply to it ; or else we must recognize an existence which, disguise it as we may, means nothing less than God.

There is no escape from this dilemma. Our choice lies between these alternatives. The sceptic will at once reject the first ; his acceptance of the second is, therefore, a

* *Descent of Man*, pt. ii. chap. xxi.

necessity. Men whose minds are enslaved by a preconceived determination to refuse belief in God, must be content here to stand like fools, owning their impotency to solve the elementary problem of existence, and, as humble disciples in the school of one Topsy, a negro slave-girl, dismissing the matter by the profound and sapient formula, "I 'spect I grow'd"! But the free thinker, unblinded by prejudice, will reject an alternative belief which is sheer credulity, and, unmoved by the sneers of pseudo-scientists and sham philosophers, will honestly and fearlessly accept the goal his reason points to, and there set up an altar to an unknown God.

CHAPTER III.

"IT'S lovely to live on a raft. We had the
sky up there all speckled with stars, and we
used to lay on our backs and look up at
them and discuss about whether they were
made, or only just happened. Jim he
allowed they was made, but I allowed they
happened ; I judged it would have took too
long to make so many. Jim said the moon
could 'a *laid* them ; well, that looked kind of
reasonable, so I didn't say nothing against
it, because I've seen a frog lay most as
many, so of course it could be done. We
used to watch the stars that fell, too, and see
them struck down. Jim allowed they'd got
spoiled and was hove out of the nest."

In this charming piece of fooling, Mark

Twain states the problem admirably. The question is whether things were made, or "only just happened." But Jim, being a philosopher, suggested evolution as a compromise, and Huck Finn's deism was not intelligent enough or vigorous enough to resist it.

"Only just happened"—that supreme folly of nineteenth-century philosophy, is as really a positive creed as the Mosaic cosmogony. And surely a venerable faith of any sort is preferable to a new-fangled superstition which has no rational sanction and is devoid even of that kind of respectability which antiquity can sometimes impart.

In our search after the origin of life, reason guides us in a path which leads direct to God. Nor let any one here object that this is but a veiled appeal to revelation. Unless reason points to the existence of a God, the question of a revelation cannot even arise. And if any one should raise the difficulty which robbed Professor Tyndall of his sleep in childhood, "Who made God?"* the solution is to be found, not in attempting to answer the question, but in exposing its absurdity. It is because science leads us back to an existence which never had a beginning, that, for want of any other term by which to designate it, we call it God.

But here we must turn back upon the ground already traversed. We have been dealing hitherto with evolution, not as an hypothesis to account for the origin of species, but merely as a pretended explanation of the origin of life ; and we have found that, thus regarded, it is but a blind lane which leads nowhere. The inquiry suggests itself, therefore, whether the conception of

---

* "Athwart all play and amusement a thread of seriousness ran through my character ; and many a sleepless night of my childhood has been passed fretted by the question; 'Who made God?'"—*Professor Virchow and Evolution.* Was the elder Mill the author of this absurd problem? See J. S. Mill's *Autobiography*, p. 43.

God be a true one which we have thus
reached by escape from a wrong path. The
question whether there be a God is no longer
open. What concerns us now is merely to
decide what kind of God we shall acknowledge. Shall we be content with the mystic
Pantheism which a false system of biology
would offer us, or shall we adore an intelligent
Ruler of the universe?

The man who can give no account of his
own existence is a fool; and he who denies
a God can give no account of his existence.
In the old time men whispered their folly
within their own hearts; nowadays they pro-
claim it on the house-tops, or, to translate the
Oriental figure into its Western correlative,
they publish it in printed books. But philosophy is not folly, and folly has no right to
call itself wisdom. There is a God—that is
certain: what then can reason tell us of
Him?

As heathen poets wrote two thousand

years ago, " We are also His offspring." *   It
behoves us, therefore, to ascribe to Him the
highest qualities which His creatures are
endowed with.   To admit, under pressure of
facts which we can neither deny nor ignore,
the conception of a God, and then to mini-
mise that conception so that it becomes inadequate to account for the facts—this is
neither reason nor philosophy, but crass folly.
Since reason shuts us up to belief in God,
let us have the courage of free thought, and
instead of taking refuge in a vague theism,
let us acknowledge a real God, a personal
God—not the great "primordial germ," but
the Creator of the heavens and the earth.

Regarded as a theory to account for life,
evolution is the wildest folly ; but as an
hypothesis to account for the varied forms of
life, it claims a hearing on its merits.   And
viewed in this light, no one need denounce it

* τοῦ γὰρ καὶ γένos ἐσμέν (Aratus, *Phæn.*) ; and Kleanthes
writes, ἐκ σοῦ γὰρ γένos ἐσμέν.

as necessarily irreligious. As the apostle of evolution with fairness urges, he who thus denounces it "is bound to show why it is more irreligious to explain the origin of man as a distinct species by descent from some lower form, through the laws of variation and natural selection, than to explain the birth of the individual through laws of ordinary reproduction. The birth both of the species and of the individual are equally parts of that grand sequence of events which our minds refuse to accept as the result of blind chance. The understanding revolts at such a conclusion." *

Mr. Darwin might, indeed, have stated the matter much more strongly. To call into existence a lowly organized form of life, endowed with latent capacities so wonderful, and so exquisitely adjusted that only when a certain stage of development is reached, the moral qualities spring into exercise, immortality is attained, and there arises in the mind

* *The Descent of Man*, pt. ii. chap. xxi.

"the idea of a universal and beneficent Creator of the universe"*—this is a far more amazing act of creative power than the Mosaic account of the genesis of man supposes. But, on the other hand, this very admission suggests a question the importance of which none but the superficial and the ignorant will doubt, Is not the Mosaic account, for that very reason, the more philosophical hypothesis?

It is obvious that when once we acknowledge "a beneficent Creator of the universe," the existence of man is explained by the necessary admission that he is a creature; and no theory of development from a lower form of life would be tenable for a moment, were it not for reasons which lie hidden, and do not appear upon the surface. Of that very character, however, are the grounds upon which the hypothesis of evolution rests. These may be summarised in a single sen-

* *The Descent of Man*, pt. ii. chap. xxi.

tence, as "the close similarity between man and the lower animals in embryonic development, as well as in innumerable points of structure and constitution, both of high and of the most trifling importance—the rudiments which he retains, and the abnormal reversions to which he is occasionally liable." *

But these facts, indisputable and striking though they be, may one and all be accounted for by an hypothesis of an exactly opposite character. Instead of assuming that the protoplastic organism was of the humblest form, but endowed with capacities of development, why should we not suppose that man himself was the primordial creature, and that he came from the Creator's hand stamped with characteristics "in innumerable points of structure and constitution," to warn him that he was made liable to a law of degeneration and decay, and that the neglect or perversion of his noble powers would degrade him inde-

* *The Descent of Man.*

finitely in the scale of life? It is certain that
this hypothesis is more in accordance with
the traditional beliefs of the heathen world
than that of evolution, and it would be easy
to maintain that it is more philosophical.*

We shall gain nothing by misrepresenting
facts, and no fair person will pretend that
experience warrants the hypothesis that any
race of men, that any individual even, ever
advanced in the scale of life save under the
constant pressure of favouring circumstances.
But while culture alone will, so far as our
experience teaches us, account for an advance,
the tendency to degenerate seems universal.
"In the Australian bush," for example, "and
in the backwoods of America, the Anglo-

* Paleontology will here be appealed to in opposition to
my suggestion, but the answer is obvious. From an age
when the earth was thinly populated, and extreme respect
was shown to the dead, we could not expect to find fossil
human remains unless we suppose that the geological strata
in which the fossils are found were formed in sudden con-
vulsions of nature, and this supposition would put Paleontology out of court altogether.

Saxon race, in which civilization has developed the higher feelings to a considerable degree, rapidly lapses into comparative barbarism, adopting the moral code, and sometimes the habits, of savages." *

And evolution, while in theory at least accounting for the physical facts it appeals to, makes no reasonable attempt to explain the moral phenomena which claim our attention, though these are far more significant and important. We know what it is to meet with people over whose origin or career some mystery evidently hangs. A *bar sinister* has crossed their pedigree, or their life is darkened by some strange secret. And is there not something akin to this in the history of our race? Can any intelligent observer look back upon the history of the world, or honestly face the dismal facts of life around us—"the turbid ebb and flow of human misery," and fail to find traces of some mysterious disaster

* *Principles of Biology*, § 67.

in primeval times, which still disturbs the moral sphere?

According to the evolutionist, man is but an upstart, a biological *parvenu*, ever in danger of betraying his humble origin, and occasionally showing a tendency to revert to his former state. But surely it is only a base materialism which would assign to the phenomena on which this theory rests, the same importance as that which we ascribe to the mysteries of man's inner being. The presence in embryo of organs properly belonging to the brute, or such "reversions" as "the occasional appearance of canine teeth"—what are these in comparison with the fact that life from the cradle to the grave is marked by baffled aspirations after an unattainable ideal, and unsatisfied cravings for the infinite? Are we to believe that these cravings and aspirations are derived from the "hairy quadruped with a tail and pointed ears?"

"Man," the evolutionist declares, "still

bears in his bodily frame the indelible stamp of his lowly origin." * His inner being, we may with greater truth reply, gives unmistakable proof that his origin was a high and noble one. Evolution, remember, is not fact, but only theory. The facts are the pearls; evolution is but the string on which we are asked to hang them. And we shall seek in vain for a single shred of direct evidence in support of it.†

It is significant that naturalists who suppose new species to be originated by evolution "habitually suppose the origination to occur in some region remote from human observation." ‡ These results are supposed to have been produced during "those im-

* These are the closing words of *The Descent of Man.*

† I am aware that Mr. Herbert Spencer asserts that the hypothesis "has the support of direct evidence" (*Principles of Biology*, § 121). But this extraordinary statement can be accounted for only by supposing that he uses words in a loose and popular way which cannot be permitted here.

‡ The language, but not the application of it, is Mr. Herbert Spencer's (*Principles of Biology*, § 112).

measurable epochs," "untold millions of
years" before "beings endowed with capacity for wide thought" existed on the earth.*
To which the sceptic will make answer:
First, that there is no proof that this earth
has so long existed in a habitable state; it
is a mere inference based upon a certain
geological theory which is wholly unproved
and by no means universally accepted. And,
secondly, that as neither the course of nature
within known periods, nor the skill of man,
has ever produced a species, we may be
merely stultifying our minds by dismissing
the difficulty to a mythical past about which
we may conjecture and romance, but con-
cerning which we know absolutely nothing.

But let us for the moment recognize these
"untold millions of years," these "immea-
surable epochs" of an "abysmal past," during
which the evolutionary process has been
developing. Further, let us concede that the

* *Principles of Biology*, §§ 114, 120.

supposed process is so slow that no appreci-
able change may be looked for within the
period of historic time. In fact, let us, for
the sake of argument, admit everything
assumed by the evolutionist, excepting only
the hypothesis of evolution itself, and we can
at once subject that hypothesis to a practical
test of the simplest kind, which will either
establish its truth or demonstrate its falseness.

Suppose our world were visited by a being
of intelligence, able to converse with men,
but wholly ignorant of an existence like ours,
marked by development and decay. Brought
face to face with puling infancy, vigorous
manhood, and the senile decrepitude of extreme old age, such a being might express
incredulous wonder on hearing that these
were but successive stages in human life.
And he might answer fairly and with shrewd-
ness, " If such a statement be true, then there
must be individuals in the world of every
possible age, from a minute to a hundred

D

years, and manifesting every imaginable degree of growth and decline." To which the unequivocal reply we should of course be able to offer would put an end to his scepticism.

But suppose we were to make some such answer as this: "True it is that never a moment passes but that some new life enters the world, and some blighted or withered life disappears from it; the processes of generation and growth and decay are all unceasing and constant; but yet we cannot satisfy the test you put to us. We can show you large children and small adults, smooth-faced boys and full-bearded men, types of failing manhood and of hale old age, but there are 'missing links' which we cannot supply. Of some of these we have 'archeological evidence,' there are fossil specimens in our museums; and the learned tell us that others no doubt exist and will yet be found; but of living specimens there are none, though all the resources of nature and of science have been appealed to in the effort to produce them." With such an answer our ephemeral visitor might well return to his celestial home perplexed with grave misgivings respecting our honesty or our intelligence.

And so here. The cases are entirely parallel. If the process of evolution have been in operation during infinite æons of time, and be still at work, " missing links " are out of the question. The naturalist will, of course, be able to point to types of every imaginable stage of development, from the simplest and humblest to the most exquisitely complex and perfect. But the naturalist can do no such thing. There are almost innumerable gaps in the chain, which could only be accounted for by the supposition that the process of evolution has again and again been interrupted during intervals so prolonged, that in comparison with them the entire period of historic time is but as a tick of the clock. Therefore it is that at every step the naturalist has to appeal to the Paleontologist. As Professor Huxley will tell us, "The only perfectly safe foundation for the doctrine of evolution lies in the historical, or rather archeological evidence, that particular organisms have arisen by the gradual modification of their predecessors, which is furnished by fossil remains."

The evolutionist professes to account for the origin of species, but, finding as he proceeds that, under his hypothesis, the problem remains inexplicable, he strives to conceal its real character. Whence the distinctions which he thus classifies? How can he account for species itself? He struggles to escape from the difficulty by representing all such distinctions as being purely arbitrary. But such a piece of "special pleading" only betrays the weakness of his position. The lines which separate one species from another are clearly marked, as is evidenced by the undoubted fact that the effects alike of culture and neglect are strictly limited by them. The reality of the difficulty, moreover, the evolutionist himself acknowledges by the recognition of missing links, and by his appeal to the fossils to supply them. The necessity for the admission and the appeal are a conclusive proof that his hypothesis is false.*

* But it may be said, these objections also apply to the rival hypothesis of degeneration. Perhaps they do, but by no means to the same extent. And if, accepting the facts to which evolution appeals, we reverse the supposed process, we shall escape from other difficulties altogether. Under the received theory, for example, the effect is always greater than the cause ; but here the cause is greater than the effect. To take one signal instance, it is surely more philosophical to suppose that immortality, and a belief in God, are lost by creatures who sink, than that they are gained by creatures who rise, in the scale of development.

CHAPTER IV.

THE hypothesis of degeneration has been here suggested as a rival to that of evolution. It equally accounts for the facts, and is less beset with difficulties. Are we, then, to accept it? By no means. Both alike are mere theories, wholly unsupported by direct evidence; and therefore the sceptic will reject both, unless they be alternatives, and he is thus compelled to make choice between them. But they are not alternatives. The facts submitted to our notice by the naturalist would be still more fully accounted for by the assumption that every kind of creature sprang from the same Creator's hand.

And this is, in fact, the only alternative which the evolutionist admits. " We have to choose between two hypotheses," he tells us—"the hypothesis of special creations, and the hypothesis of evolution." The necessity for this admission, be it observed, is by implication a conclusive proof that evolution is unproved.*

Let us, then, consider the suggested alternative. Mr. Herbert Spencer will tell us that, "however regarded, the hypothesis of special creations turns out to be worthless— worthless by its derivation; worthless in its intrinsic incoherence; worthless as absolutely without evidence; worthless as not supplying an intellectual need; worthless as not satisfying a moral want. We must, therefore," he concludes, "consider it as counting for nothing in opposition to any other hypothesis respecting the origin of organic beings." †

Upon the legal mind the effect of this

* It is only where there is no direct proof that a result has been caused in one way that we need to show it could not have occurred in any other way (see p. 9, *ante*).

† *Principles of Biology*, § 115.

sort of onslaught is merely to excite suspicion that some weak point in the case requires to be concealed. Such dogmatism of assertion must only serve to encourage us in our investigation of the argument.

First, then, we are told that the notion of a creation is a primitive one, and "early ideas are not usually true ideas." * But this is a very transparent *petitio principii;* for unless we assume that evolution is true, which is precisely what has to be proved, the statement is of no force whatever.

Mr. Herbert Spencer proceeds to urge that a belief in creation is discredited by "association with a special class of mistaken beliefs." † Now this, of course, is a reference to the Mosaic account of the creation, ‡ and it is

---

* *Principles of Biology*, § 110.   † *Ib.*, § 111.

‡ For there is no other record of primitive beliefs in question here. Mr. Spencer, it is true, seeks to create a prejudice by bracketing it with "the cosmogony of the Indians or the Greeks." At the Bar this would be characterized as a *nisi prius* trick.

sufficiently answered by the fact that that account is accepted by many men of competent attainments and of the highest intellectual capacity. *

Again, we are told that not only is this hypothesis "not countenanced by a single fact," but further, that it "cannot be framed into a coherent thought," † and "is merely a formula for our ignorance." ‡ "No one ever saw a special creation." § True : but a similar objection may be made to the hypothesis of evolution ; and it has, in fact, been urged in these pages in the very words here used by Mr. Herbert Spencer.‖ It is admitted that no new species has ever been evolved within human experience, and the supposed origination is referred to "an

---

* They are careful, no doubt, to distinguish between what the Patriarch actually taught, and what, as they maintain, a crude misapprehension of his teaching attributes to him. But this does not affect my argument.

† *Principles of Biology*, § 112.   ‡ *Ib.*, § 113.

§ *Ib.*, § 112.   ‖ See pp. 13, 14, *ante.*

abysmal past," which may, for aught we know, be purely fabulous. The objection, if of force at all, is equally valid against both hypotheses.

For let us keep clearly in view what our author studiously conceals, that at this point the real question is not the origin of species, but the origin of life. Until he can give us some reasonable account of the existence of life, we shall continue to believe in "a beneficent Creator of the universe;" and though Mr. Herbert Spencer will deplore our "ignorance" and despise our "pseud-ideas," we shall console ourselves by the companionship of a long line of illustrious men, whose names perchance shall be increasingly venerated in the world of philosophy and letters when some new generation of scientists shall have arisen to regard with patronising pity the popular theories of to-day.

"No one ever saw a special creation," and the hypothesis "cannot be framed into a coherent thought." This implies, first, an admission that if we were permitted to see a special creation we could frame the coherent thought ; and, secondly, an implied assertion that our ability to frame ideas is limited by our experience. The admission is fatal, and the assertion is obviously false.

Mr. Herbert Spencer's remaining objections to special creations are an enumeration of certain theological difficulties, in which those who espouse the hypothesis are supposed to entangle themselves.*   These might be dismissed with the remark that a mere *ad hominem* argument is of no importance here. If valid, it could only serve to discredit theology, without strengthening the author's position.   But let us examine it.

The objections are briefly these. Theology is supposed to teach that special creations were designed to demonstrate to mankind the power of the Creator : " would it not have been still better demonstrated by the sepa-

* *Principles of Biology*, § 114.

rate creation of each individual?" It is quite unnecessary to discuss this, for there is not a suggestion in the Bible from cover to cover that creation had any such purpose.* What evolution assumes,† the Bible asserts, namely, that man did not appear in the world until after every other organized form was already in existence.

But the next and final difficulty appears at first sight to be more serious. "Omitting the human race, for whose defects and miseries the current theology professes to account, and limiting ourselves to the lower creation, what must we think of the countless different pain-inflicting appliances and instincts with which animals are endowed?"‡ "Whoever con-

* When a writer speaks of theology in general terms, without indicating any particular author or school, it must be assumed that he refers to the Bible, which is, of course, the only religious book that all educated readers are supposed to be familiar with.

† I do not assert that all evolutionists admit this, but I maintain that it is implied in the hypothesis of evolution.

‡ *Principles of Biology*, § 114.

tends that each kind of animal was specially
designed, must assert either that there was a
deliberate intention on the part of the Creator
to produce these results, or that there was an
inability to prevent them." This difficulty,
moreover, is greatly intensified by the fact
that "of the animal kingdom as a whole,
more than half the species are parasites, and
thus we are brought to the contemplation of
innumerable cases in which the suffering
inflicted brings no compensating benefit."

Now, in the first place, these objections are
applicable as really, though, perhaps, not to
the same extent, to the hypothesis of creation
in general ; and, as we have seen, that hypothesis is no longer in question. And, in the
second place, we must remember that these
difficulties are purely theological. They have
no force save against those who believe the
Bible. Such people, according to the argument, must abandon either the Biblical
account of creation or the Biblical represen-

tation of God.   They must assert either that
the Creator intended to produce the results
here under observation, or that there was an
inability to prevent them.   In other words,
God is deficient either in goodness or in
power.

This, of course, introduces a question which
hitherto has been studiously avoided in these
pages.   Nor shall it here receive more than
the briefest notice ; for even a conventional
acquaintance with the biblical scheme will
enable us to find the solution of Mr. Herbert
Spencer's difficulties.   The validity of his
dilemma depends upon ignoring one of the
fundamental dogmas of theology.   The teaching of the Bible is unmistakable, that Adam
in his fall dragged down with him the entire
creation of which he was the federal head ;
that the suffering under which the creature
groans is not the result of design, but of a
tremendous catastrophe which has brought
ruin and misery in its train ; that the Creator

is not wanting in power to restore creation to its pristine perfectness ; that He has pledged Himself to accomplish this very result, and that so complete will be the restoration, that even the destructive propensities of the brute shall absolutely cease.

Such is the teaching of theology, unfolded not merely in the poetry of the Hebrew prophets, but in the dogmatic prose of the Apostle of the Gentiles. The question here is not whether it be reasonable, whether it be true. All that concerns us is the fact that it forms an essential part of the biblical scheme, and thus affords a complete refutation of an *ad hominem* argument which depends for its validity upon misrepresenting or ignoring it.

Mr. Herbert Spencer's indictment against belief in special creations thus begins and ends by disingenuous attempts to prejudice the issue. And in asserting that the hypothesis is incapable of being " framed into a coherent thought," he urges an objection which from its very nature admits of no other answer than that which has been already given to it. If we call for a poll upon the question, we shall find on one side a crowd of illustrious men of unquestionable fame and of the very highest rank as philosophers and thinkers ; and, on the other, Mr. Herbert Spencer and a few more besides, all of whom must await the verdict of posterity, before they can be permanently assigned the place which their contemporaries possibly would claim for them. An assertion which thus brands the entire bead-roll of philosophers, from Bacon to Charles Darwin, as the dupes of a "pseud-idea," a "formula for ignorance," is worthless, save as affording matter for a psychological study of a most interesting kind.

The alleged absence of evidence of a special creation has been already met by pointing out that the objection equally applies to the hypothesis of evolution. But perhaps it deserves a fuller notice. "No one ever saw a special creation," we are told. The author might have added that if the entire Royal Society in council were permitted to "see a special creation," the sceptic would reject their testimony unless there were indirect evidence to confirm it. In the sphere of the miraculous, direct evidence, unless thus confirmed, is of no value at second hand. Produce for our inspection the organism alleged to have been created, and satisfy us, first, that it had no existence prior to the moment assigned for its creation, and, secondly, that it could not have originated in some way known to our experience, and then, indeed, we shall give up our scepticism and accept the testimony offered us.

But Mr. Herbert Spencer goes on to aver that "no one ever found proof of an indirect kind that a special creation had taken place." This is a choice example of the *nisi prius* artifice at which our author is such an adept.

E

The existence of a world teeming with life
has been accepted by the greatest and wisest
men of every age as a conclusive proof that
a special creation has taken place. But this
is boldly met by sheer weight of unsupported
denial.

If we approach the subject, not as special
pleaders or partisans, but in a philosophic
spirit, we shall state the argument thus :—
The admitted facts give proof that species
originated either by special creations or by
evolution. If either hypothesis can be established by independent evidence, the other
is thereby discredited. But, in the one case
as in the other, positive proof is wholly wanting. We must, therefore, rely upon general
considerations. On the evolution theory,
proof is confessedly wanting that the alleged
cause is adequate to account for the admitted
facts.* Not so on the creation hypothesis, for

* I do not say there is no *evidence*. But all admit that
that evidence does not amount to proof, unless, indeed, the

as we admit that *life* originated by creation,* there can be no difficulty in assigning a similar origin to species. In a word, as we believe in "a beneficent Creator of the universe," the evolution hypothesis is unnecessary and therefore unphilosophical.

But, further, the concealed consequences of the argument under review must not be overlooked. If it be valid for any purpose at all, it disproves not only the fact of a creation, but the existence of a Creator. "No one ever saw a special creation :" neither did any one ever see the Deity. If, as alleged, we have no evidence of His handiwork, neither have we proof of His existence. At a single plunge we have thus reached the level of blank atheism, which is the extreme depth of moral and intellectual degradation. "The birth both of the species and the individual "

alternative hypothesis can be disproved ; and to disprove it is the whole point and purpose of Mr. Herbert Spencer's chapter on the subject.

* See pp. 22–24, *ante.*

must equally be ascribed to " blind chance,"
" coercion " being appealed to, I suppose, to
quell the inevitable " revolt of the understanding." *   And the strange religious propensities
common to the race, whether civilised or
savage, must also be suppressed ; or, at all
events, our *Penates* must be strictly limited to
an effigy of our hairy quadrumanous ancestor
with pointed ears, supplemented possibly by
some " symbolic conception " of the primordial
life-germ wrapped in cloud, and a copy of
Mr. Herbert Spencer's " System of Philosophy " to guide and regulate the *culte !*

* See p. 25, *ante.*

CHAPTER V.

SCEPTICISM is " not a permanent resting-place for human reason." The knowledge that there is bad money in circulation does not make us fling our purse into the gutter, or refuse to replenish it when empty. The sceptic tries a coin before accepting it, but when once he puts it in his pocket, his appreciation of it is, for that very reason, all the more intelligent and full. A convinced doubter makes the best believer.

With an open mind and unwavering confidence the true sceptic acknowledges a personal God, " the beneficent Creator of the universe." And in no grudging spirit, but honestly and fully, he will own the obligations and relationships which this involves. Religion is implied in the acknowledgment of God. And further, this acknowledgment removes every *a priori* objection to the idea of a revelation. Some perhaps might urge that it creates a positive presumption in its favour. If, indeed, we are the offspring of a "beneficent Creator," is it not improbable that, in a world so darkened by sorrow and doubt, He would leave us without guidance, and without light as to our destiny?

At all events, our belief in God makes it incumbent on us to examine any alleged revelation which is presented to us with reasonable credentials. If some one bring me what purports to be a message or letter from my brother, I may dispose of the matter by answering, "I have no brother;" but if I possess an unknown lost brother, I cannot refuse to receive the communication, and to test its claims on my attention.

But here we must keep our heads. There

is no sphere in which the functions of the constable are more needed. The existence of a lost brother is no reason for sheltering impostors. Our belief in God is no reason for abandoning ourselves to superstition, or submitting to be duped by foolish or designing men.

Yet another caution is needed here. We have now reached ground where the judgment of men of science is of no special value whatever. So long as it is a question of investigating and describing the facts and phenomena of nature, we sit at their feet with unfeigned admiration of their genius and industry ; but when it becomes a question of adjudicating upon the proofs they furnish us with, they must give way to those whose training and habits of mind make them better fitted for the task. We place the very highest value upon their evidence as experts in all matters within their own province, but we cannot consent to their passing from the witness-box to the judicial bench; least of all can we consent to their occupying such a position, where the subject-matter is one of which they have no special cognizance.* In such a case a dozen city merchants, with a trained lawyer to guide their deliberations, would make a better tribunal than the Royal Society could supply.

The extreme point to which reason leads us is the recognition of an unknown God. What now concerns us is the inquiry whether He has revealed himself to men. Have we a revelation? A discussion of this question on *a priori* lines would have many advantages. But, on the whole, the practical view of it is the best. And here it would be mere pedantry to ignore the peculiar claims which

* The childlike faith of those who so recently bowed before that false god *Bathybius Haeckeli*, puts to blush the sweet simplicity of the Sunday-school. It may seem ungenerous to remind "philosophers" of their folly, but we cannot ignore it when considering their claims to guide our judgment.

Christianity has upon our notice. In fact, the question narrows itself at once to this plain issue, Is Christianity a Divine revelation? If this question be answered in the negative, it is really useless to discuss the merits of Islam; and as for Buddha, his popularity in certain quarters in England as a rival to Christ is proof only of the depth of Saxon silliness. There is a sense, of course, in which all enthusiasm is inspiration, but for our present purpose this is a mere fencing with words. The question is perfectly definite and clear to every one who wishes to understand it, Is Christianity a revelation from God? Let us examine the witnesses.

If we ask in what form this alleged revelation comes to us, all Christians are agreed in placing in our hands a Book; in a word, they point us to the Bible. But here, at the very threshold, their unanimity ceases. While some would insist that this is the only revela-

tion, the majority of Christendom would point
us also to a certain class of men so supernaturally gifted and accredited that they are
themselves a revelation. This system, which
is historically associated with Rome, deserves
priority of consideration because of the
prestige it enjoys by reason of the antiquity
of its origin, and the influence and numbers
of its disciples. Moreover, if its claims be
accepted, the truth of Christianity is established; and if on examination they be rejected,
the ground is cleared for the consideration of
the main question on its merits.

The founders of Christianity, we are told,
in addition to their ability to work miracles
such as the senses could take notice of,
possessed also supernatural powers of a
mystic kind. By certain mystic rites, for
instance, they were able to bring human
beings into immediate relationship with the
Deity, or to work such a transformation in
common bread and ordinary wine, that,

although no available test could detect the change, the bread really became flesh, and the wine blood. Further still, we are assured that these powers have been transmitted from generation to generation, and are now possessed by the successors of the men who first received them direct from Heaven. And more than this, we are asked to believe that these miracles are actually performed in our own day, not in isolated and remote places far removed from observation, but in our midst and everywhere ; and that, too, in the most public and open manner. We have but to present our infant children to one of these men, and he can establish between them and God a spiritual relationship akin to that created naturally by generation, and in fact described as re-generation.

If this be true, it is obvious that not only the miracles which are thus wrought in our presence, but the very men themselves who cause them, are a Divine revelation. We

are no longer left to reach out toward the
Supreme Being by the light of reason; we
are thus brought face to face with God.

Indifference is impossible in the presence
of such demands on our faith. If these men
in fact possess such powers, it is difficult to
set a limit to the respect and veneration due
to them. But if their pretensions be false, it
is monstrous that they should be permitted
to trade upon the credulity of mankind.
To enable us to grapple at once with the
immediate issue here involved, it is worth
while to make any admission necessary.
Let us admit the truth of Christianity, and,
further still, let us admit that the apostles
possessed the powers which are here in
question. Admitting all this, are these
powers in fact possessed by the men who
now claim to exercise them?

It is not easy to decide what amount of
evidence ought to be deemed sufficient in
such a case. But is there any evidence at

all? These powers are not supposed to be
conferred immediately from Heaven, but
mediately through other men, who in turn
had received them from their predecessors,
and so on in an unbroken line extending
back to the days of the apostles. No man
who is satisfied with the evidence upon which
evolution rests can fairly dispute the proofs
of an apostolic succession. Let us, therefore,
go so far in our admissions as even to accept
this also; and that, too, without stopping to
investigate the lives of those through whom
the "succession" flowed. Some of them
were famous for their piety, others were in-
famous for their crimes. But passing all this
by, let us get face to face with the living men
who make these amazing demands upon our
faith.

And, in order to avoid collateral issues, let
us confine the inquiry to the claim they make
to be able to cause the spiritual regeneration
of human beings, who are thus, on certain

highly reasonable conditions, secured an eter-
nity of blessedness.   Some of these men were
our playmates in early childhood, and our
class-fellows and companions in school and
college days.   We recall their friendly rivalry
in our studies and our sports, and their share
in many a debauch that now we no longer
speak of when we meet.   Some of them are
the firm and valued friends of our manhood.
We respect them for their learning, and still
more for their piety and their self-denying
efforts for the good of their fellow-men.
Others, again, have fallen from our acquaintance.   Although, *ex hypothesi*, equally endowed with supernatural gifts which should
make us value their presence at our death-
bed, they are exceptionally addicted to
natural vices which lead us to shun them in
our lifetime.

And this disposes of one ground on which
possibly a *primâ facie* case might be set up.
If all those who are supposed to possess

these extraordinary powers were distinguished from their fellow-men by high and noble qualities, their pretensions would at least deserve our respect. So, also, if this were true of those in whom they profess to work the miracle of regeneration. But, in the one case as in the other, we fail to find any special marks of character or conduct, which even the most partial judge could point to for such a purpose.

What other kind of proofs, then, can we look for? It is idle to beat about the bush. The fact is clear as light that there is not a shadow of evidence of any description whatsoever to support these claims. This being so, we must at once recall one of the admissions already made, lest these men should take refuge in an appeal to the New Testament as establishing their position. The enlightened Christianity of the Reformation emphatically denies that even the apostles possessed such powers, or that the Bible gives any countenance whatever to the assumption of them. In a word, Christians themselves, and these the very *élite* of Christendom, maintain that all such priestly pretensions have no foundation save in medieval superstition.

If Christianity be true, if the Bible be inspired, we need not hesitate to believe that certain men are divinely called and qualified as religious teachers. But this position is separated by an impassable gulf from the mystic pretensions of priestcraft. In truth, sacerdotalism presents extraordinary problems for the consideration of the thoughtful. If it prevailed only among the ignorant and degraded, it would deserve no attention. But the fact is beyond question that its champions and votaries include men of the highest intellectual eminence and moral worth. The integrity of such men is irreproachable. They are not accomplices in a wilful fraud upon their fellows; they are true and honest in their convictions. How, then, are we to account for the fact that many who hold such high rank as scholars and thinkers are thus the dupes of a delusion so utterly base and silly? How is it to be explained that here in England, while we boast of increasing enlightenment, this delusion is regaining its hold upon the religious life of the nation? The national Church, which half a century ago was comparatively free from the evil, is now hopelessly leavened with it. The more this matter be studied the more inexplicable it seems, unless we are prepared to believe in the existence of spiritual influences of a sinister kind, by which in the religious sphere the minds even of men of intellect and culture are liable to be warped and blinded.

F

CHAPTER VI.

Is Christianity a Divine revelation? This
question must not be settled by the result of
the preliminary inquiry here proposed. In
rejecting sacerdotalism as a degrading medieval superstition, we merely clear the ground
for a discussion of the main question upon
its merits. "The Reformation," says Mr.
Goldwin Smith, "was a tremendous earth-
quake" which "shook down the fabric of
medieval religion." "But," he goes on to
say, "it left the authority of the Bible un-
shaken, and men might feel that the destructive process had its limit, and that adamant
was still beneath their feet."

To the Bible, then, we turn. But how is

such an inquiry to be conducted? The un-
fairness of entrusting the defence of Christianity to any who are themselves the rejecters
of Christianity will be palpable to every one.
Here the right of audience is only to the
Christian. But, in making this concession,
the sceptic may fairly insist on maintaining
the place of critic, if not of censor. Until
convinced, he will continue to consider, reflect, hesitate, doubt.

And it is a suspicious circumstance that so
many who claim to be leaders of religious
thought, and who are professional exponents
of the Christian faith, seem eager not only to
eliminate from Christianity everything that is
distinctive, but also to divorce it from much
with which, in its origin, it was inseparably
associated. They are strangely anxious to
separate it from the Judaism which it suc-
ceeded, and upon which it is so indisputably
founded. As a corollary upon this, they
struggle to separate the New Testament from

the Old, treating the Hebrew Scriptures, and
especially the Pentateuch, as persons who
have risen in the world are prone to treat
the *quondam* acquaintances of humbler days.
As a further step, they betray unmistakable
uneasiness when confronted with the miraculous in the Bible ; and "the old evangelical
doctrine" of inspiration they regard with
undisguised dislike, if not contempt.

No well-informed person will dispute that
this is a fair statement of the position assumed
by a school of religious thought, which is in
its own sphere as influential and popular as
is that which identifies itself with sacerdotalism.   But they who hold such ground as
this are trading far too recklessly upon our
supposed ignorance of the Bible.   They forget
that it is the most ancient book in the world,
and that our "Authorised Version" is the
greatest of English classics.   Many even of
those who reject its claims to transcendental
reverence are well versed in its contents.

And it needs no more than a conventional knowledge of the New Testament to enable us to assert that the Christianity of Christ and His apostles was *not* a new religion, but merely an unfolding and fulfilment of the Judaism which preceded it. The Christ of Christendom was a crucified Jew—crucified because He declared Himself to be the Jews' Messiah; and with that Messiahship is inseparably connected His only claims upon our homage and our faith.

And what were the credentials of His Messiahship? To some extent the miracles which He wrought, but mainly the Hebrew Scriptures. And in His appeal to those Scriptures He implicitly asserted that they were in the strictest and, as we should term it, the narrowest sense, inspired. Ten times are those Scriptures quoted in the first four chapters of the New Testament as being the *ipsissima verba* of the Deity,* and three of

* The friend who has aided me here calls my attention to

these quotations are from the very book which these Christian theologians are most eager to separate themselves from, namely, the Book of Deuteronomy.

The language of the "Sermon on the Mount" is, if possible, more emphatic still. To understand its full significance we must bear in mind what Josephus asserts, that by all Jews the Scriptures "were justly believed to be Divine, so that, rather than speak against them, they were ready to suffer torture or even death." * It was to a people saturated with this belief that such words as the following were spoken: "Think not that I am come to destroy the law, or the prophets : I am not come to destroy, but to fulfil. For verily I say unto you, Till heaven and earth pass, one jot or one tittle shall in no wise pass from the law, till

the force of διa in such passages as Matt. i. 22 as emphasized by the Revised Version : "That it might be fulfilled which was spoken *by* the Lord *through* the prophet."

* Josephus, *Apion*, i. 8.

all be fulfilled." "The 'jot' (we are told) is
the Greek *iota*, the Hebrew *yod*, the smallest
of all the letters of the alphabet. The ' tittle '
was one of the smallest strokes or twists of
other letters." What language, then, could
possibly assert more plainly that, so far from
coming to set up a new religion, as these
Christian teachers would tell us, the Nazarene
declared His mission to be the recognition and
fulfilment of the old Hebrew Scriptures in
every part, even to the minutest detail?

And all that is distinctly miraculous in
those Scriptures was specially adopted in His
teaching; as, for example, Noah's deluge; the
destruction of Sodom and Gomorrah ; Jonah
and the fish ; Moses and the burning bush ;
the Heaven-sent manna in the wilderness ;
Elijah's raising the widow's son from the
dead ; the cure of Naaman's leprosy by
bathing in the Jordan.

The dilemma in which this places the
Christian is inexorable. If Christ was Divine,

the truth of everything adopted and accredited by His teaching is placed beyond question. To plead that, with a view to advance His Messianic claims, He pandered to Jewish ignorance and prejudice, is not only to admit that He was merely human, but to endanger our respect for Him even as a Rabbi. And yet Christian teachers have the temerity to suggest such an explanation of His words. Such a position is utterly illogical, if not positively dishonest. The Christian is, to borrow a legal term, *estopped* from questioning the inspiration of the Old Testament, or the reality of the miracles recorded in it; and when we find teachers who call themselves Christians and yet question both, we cannot hesitate to conclude that their position is utterly untenable, betokening either flagrant dishonesty, or else credulity as thorough as the faith of the sacerdotalist.

But, it may be urged, it is not the teaching of Christ which is disparaged, but only the record of that teaching. It is here that allowance must be made for Jewish ignorance and prejudice. That the Jews believed their Scriptures to be inspired is admitted, and therefore it was that those who chronicled the words of Christ gave that colour to His doctrine. The New Testament is marked by the same imperfections as the Old. It is of priceless value as the record of Divine facts, but it is upon those facts themselves, and not upon the record of them, that Christianity is founded.

This answer is plausible, but upon examination it will prove to be absolutely fatal. It is, no doubt, the teaching of Christ, as recorded in the Gospels, which alone renders it imperative upon the Christian to believe in the inspiration of the Hebrew Scriptures. But when we turn to the Gospels themselves, we find that of necessity the whole fabric of Christianity stands or falls with our acceptance or rejection of their claims to be, in the

strictest and fullest sense, a Divine revelation.
Most true it is that the system rests on facts,
and not on writings merely ; and this it is,
indeed, which distinguishes it from all other
religions. But such is the character of the
facts on which it is based, that if the record
of them be thus disparaged, belief in these
facts is sheer credulity. The public facts of
the ministry and death of Christ are as well
authenticated as any other events of ancient
history. No one questions them. But the
entire significance of those facts depends
upon their relation to other facts behind
them—facts of a purely transcendental character, and such as no amount of human
testimony would warrant our accepting.

Assume that after His crucifixion Christ
was seen alive by great numbers of credible
witnesses, persons who were thoroughly ac-
quainted with Him—five hundred are ex-
pressly reckoned by St. Paul—and the proof
that He was then alive would be accepted by

any tribunal in the world for any purpose whatsoever. But this, instead of availing to prove the fact of His resurrection, may serve only to disprove the reality of His death. That He seemed to die is clearly established by the fact that His executioners gave up His body. That His disciples—that He Himself—believed He had died and come to life again, there is no need to question. But, regarding the narrative of the Gospels as entirely human, the sceptic is compelled to refuse belief in the fact of His death.

But it may perhaps be answered here, that though the record was human, the Person of whom it speaks was more than human ; the whole argument, therefore, depends upon ignoring the great fundamental fact of Christianity, that Christ was Himself Divine. The rejoinder, surely, would be legitimate, that this only renders the story of His death more utterly incredible than ever. But, passing

that by, let us investigate the evidence for
His Divinity.

No effort shall be spared to present the
matter in such a way as least to offend the
susceptibilities of the believer; but nothing
can be gained by refusing to face the
question fairly. The Nazarene was admit-
tedly the son of Mary. The Jews declared
He was the son of Joseph; the Christian
worships Him as the Son of God. The
founder of Rome was said to be the divinely
begotten child of a vestal virgin. And in
the old Babylonian mysteries a similar parent-
age was ascribed to the martyred son of
Semiramis, gazetted Queen of Heaven. What
grounds have we, then, for distinguishing the
miraculous birth at Bethlehem from these and
other kindred legends of the ancient world?

To point to the resurrection is a transparent begging of the question. To appeal
to human testimony is utter folly. At this
point we are face to face with that to which

no consensus of human testimony could
lend even an *a priori* probability. To urge
that Christ disclosed the fact to His disciples does not advance the matter a single
step. Here again, then, the Christian is on
the horns of an inexorable dilemma. He
must admit that the foundation on which his
religion rests is but a Galilæan legend, or
else he must insist that the Gospels are God-
breathed writings—an authoritative revelation from Heaven. And no one who accepts
the Gospels as inspired is at liberty to doubt
the inspiration of the Old Testament, or to
question the genuineness of the miracles of
either Old Testament or New.

Whatever may be said, therefore, of the
theological school here under review, their
religion is not Christianity, and their testimony must be rejected as of less value even
than that of the sacerdotalists. Nor can any
one justly take exception to the fairness of
this argument. If we be urged to embark in

a gold-mine, we naturally ask whether those who commend it to our confidence have themselves put their money in it. Nor will this avail to satisfy us if we find that they have also invested in other undertakings which we know to be worthless. And so here: we are entitled to put men upon proof, not only of the sincerity and consistency of their faith, but also of its reasonableness. And we find that the faith of Christians of the one school includes tenets the belief in which implies mental degradation, and that the unfaith of Christians of the other school undermines Christianity altogether. The one school believes too much, the other believes too little. With the one, faith degenerates into mere superstition; with the other, it merges in a scepticism which is as real, though not as rational or consistent, as is that of many who are commonly branded as infidels.

CHAPTER VII.

"WE are without any rational ground for believing in science;" "We are without any rational ground for determining the logical relation which ought to subsist between science and religion." Such are among the startling theses maintained by the author of *A Defence of Philosophic Doubt.* And one of the main results of his argument is stated thus: "In the absence, then, of reason to the contrary, I am content," he says, "to regard the two great creeds by which we attempt to regulate our lives as resting in the main upon separate bases." A protest this against "the existence of a whole class of 'apologists' the end of whose labours appears to be to explain, or to explain away, every appearance of contradiction between the two."

But here Mr. Balfour fails of his usual precision. A definition of religion is wanting. He seems sometimes to use the word in its first and widest sense, and at other times as equivalent to a particular system of belief, and, by implication, to Christianity. A consciousness of our own existence is the foundation of all knowledge. And that elementary fact is the first stepping-stone by the aid of which we apprehend the existence of God. It might be fairly argued that our knowledge of the existence of God rests upon a surer basis than our knowledge of the external world, and therefore that religion in that sense takes precedence of science. But such a plea is unnecessary, because our knowledge of the external world is, for the practical purposes of life, absolute and un-questioned. We may be content, therefore, to assert that the two creeds stand upon a perfect equality.*

And, speaking generally, belief in both is universal. There are exceptions, doubtless— as, for example, "street arabs and advanced thinkers;" † but this does not affect the argument. Science depends on our belief in the external world; religion on our belief in God. Religious feeling springs from the relation in which we stand to a Supreme Power; and, as Professor Tyndall will tell us, "religious feeling is as much a verity as any other part of human consciousness, and against it, on its subjective side, the waves of science beat in vain." ‡

But so far we have been dealing merely with what is called natural religion. It is

---

* "My complaint rather is that of the two creeds which, from a philosophical point of view, stand, so far as I can judge, upon a perfect equality, one should be set up as a standard to which the other must necessarily conform."—*A Defence of Philosophic Doubt*, p. 303.

† *Ib.*, p. 319.　　　　‡ *Virchow and Evolution.*

G

not until we pass into the sphere of revealed religion that the seeming conflict with science arises. And the difficulties of practical men are of a wholly different order from those which perplex the philosophers. Take for example, the argument against miracles. An intelligent schoolboy can see that the solution of the problem depends on the answer we make to the question whether there be a God. Even John Stuart Mill admits this. To acknowledge the existence of a God possessed of power infinitely greater than that of man, and yet to insist that he must necessarily be a cipher in the world— this may pass for philosophy, but a different sort of word would describe it better.

And as with the so-called "laws" of science, so also is it with its theories. Excepting only the evolution craze, which enjoys an ephemeral popularity, common men care nothing for them. What weighs with earnest thinkers who are real truth-lovers is that ascertained facts appear to disprove the truth of what has been received as a Divine revelation.

But treatises such as those of which *A Defence of Philosophic Doubt* is a most striking example, are further defective in that they defend religion upon a ground which leaves the apologist equally free to fall back upon sacerdotalism or any other superstition, as to vindicate the claims of the Bible to be a revelation. And as a result of this, in discussing the foundations of belief they ignore the doctrine of transcendental faith, which is characteristic of Christianity.

The theological argument from miracles has, at least in its common form, no scientific or biblical sanction. The fact of a miracle is a proof merely of the presence of some power greater than man's. That such a power is necessarily Divine is an inference which reason refuses to accept, and Christianity very emphatically denies.*

* Scripture is explicit that miracles have been, and **may**

Every one who believes in a God must be prepared to admit that there may be creatures in the universe far superior to man in intelligence and power; and even an atheistic evolutionist would as freely admit this, if he were honest and fearless in his philosophy.* It is entirely a question of evidence.

But this we need not discuss. As regards the theologian the matter stands thus. He tells us that evil beings exist, endowed with powers adequate to the accomplishment of miracles on earth, and at the same time he maintains that the fact of a miracle is a proof of Divine intervention. It is not my province to defend Christianity against its own advocates, but nothing will be gained by discussing these problems on a false basis. I am not aware that in the New Testament

be, the result of demoniacal or Satanic agency. The Jews accounted thus for the miracles of Christ, and His answer was an appeal to the moral character of His works.

* The atheist, of course, would substitute "organism" or some kindred word for "creature."

the miracles are ever appealed to as an "evidence," save in connection with a preceding revelation to which they are referred. They seem to have accredited the Nazarene as being the promised Messiah. But "the fact is allowed," not, as Bishop Butler avers, "that Christianity was professed to be received into the world upon the belief of miracles," but that the claimant to Messiahship was rejected as a profane deceiver by the very people in whose midst the miracles were wrought.

And it is a further fact that no one of the writers of the New Testament accounts thus for his own faith, or for the faith of his converts. That their faith was an inference from their observation of miracles—that it was due to natural causes at all—is negatived in the plainest terms, and its supernatural origin and character are explicitly asserted. So long as the testimony was to the Jew, miracles abounded; but if St. Paul's ministry at Corinth and Thessalonica may be accepted as typical of his work among Gentiles, his Epistles to the Corinthians and Thessalonians emphatically disprove the idea that miracles were made the basis of his preaching. A single quotation from each will suffice. " The Jews require a sign " (he says ; that is, they claimed that the preaching should be accredited by miracles), "and the Greeks seek after wisdom" (that is, they posed as rationalists and philosophers) : "but" (he declares, in contrast with both) " we preach Christ crucified, unto the Jews a stumbling-block, and unto the Greeks foolishness ; but unto them which are called, both Jews and Greeks, Christ the Power of God, and the Wisdom of God." And to the Thessalonians he writes, "When ye received the Word of God which ye heard of us, ye received it not as the word of men, but as it is in truth the Word of God."

Now, no one who will examine these statements fairly, unbiased by the feelings of irritation which such language is calculated to excite, can fail to recognize their force and meaning. They do not indicate a belief resulting from the examination of evidences, or attained by any natural process, but a belief which is supernatural altogether. I am not defending this, but merely calling attention to it. We need to protest against the folly and dishonesty of those who adapt the teaching of Christ and His apostles to modern views, and call the name of Christian over the hybrid system thus formed. Their system may be an admirable one, but it is not *Christianity.* The Christian is supposed to have a faith which is produced and sustained supernaturally by his being brought into immediate relations with God. No one, of course, will deny that the God whose creatures we are can so speak to us that His Word shall carry with it the conviction that it is Divine. And if we demand why it is, then, that we all do not accept it, the Christian will answer by pleading human depravity, which renders a special intervention of the Divine Spirit necessary.

No one, again, will deny that formerly this part of the Christian system was generally accepted by professed Christians. But it has been given up, of course, by all who have ceased to regard the Bible as a Divine revelation. Naturally so, for the one part of the system depends on the other. None but half-crazed fanatics suppose that God speaks save through the Scriptures, and once we give up the old belief of Christendom, that the Scriptures are inspired—that they are what they claim to be, " the oracles of God "—the Christian theory of faith becomes untenable.

The question of inspiration is, in fact, the key to the entire position. Christianity stands or falls according to the conclusion we arrive at here.* Hence the special difficulty which

---

* It will not avail to urge the undoubted fact that some of the strongest and most cultured and most subtle intellects

embarrasses the consideration of the question. In litigation, a case can never come before a jury until some definite propositions are ascertained, which the one side maintains and the other side denies. But in this controversy "the issues" are never settled. The lines of attack and defence never meet. The scientist ignores the strength of the Christian's position; and the Christian, entrenched in that position, is wholly unreached by the objections and difficulties of the scientist.

A Defence of Philosophic Doubt—to revert to that treatise again for a moment—is an attempt to arbitrate between the two without joining hands with either. Its author is liable to be

of our own age and of preceding ages have accepted the Bible as being strictly and altogether God-breathed. The fact is a sufficient proof that there is nothing intrinsically *absurd* in such a belief, or in the Christian system which depends upon it. But if its truth could be thus established, we must be prepared to accept also whatever is believed by men of equal calibre and fame. But some such believe in baptismal regeneration, some in evolution, some even in atheism—for atheism is as much a positive faith as theism.

challenged thus : " If your treatise be intended
as a defence of natural religion, it is unnecessary ; for there is clearly no conflict between
science and natural religion. But if it be a
defence of revealed religion, that is, of Christianity, it is inadequate ; for you must fall
back upon the Bible as a Divine revelation,
and if you do so we will undermine your
whole position by proving that essential parts
of it are inconsistent with "—" the doctrines
of science," the scientist is sure to say, thus
destroying his entire argument, and leaving
himself helplessly at the mercy of Mr.
Balfour's pitiless logic. But if he were not
misled through mistaking his hobby for a
real horse, he would say, " inconsistent with
ascertained facts ; " and this position, if
proved, would refute Christianity altogether.

For example : the miraculous destruction
of the cities of the plain is one of the most
incredible things in Scripture. The scientist
rejects the narrative as being opposed to

science, just as, on the same ground, the African rejected the statement that water became so solid that men could walk upon it. But if the scientist could fix the site of Sodom and Gomorrah, and point to the condition of the soil as proof that no such phenomenon as is detailed in Genesis could have occurred there, the fact would be fatal not only to the authority of the Pentateuch, but to the Messianic claims of the Nazarene, who identified Himself with it. But the scientist does nothing of the kind. On the contrary, the admitted facts are consistent with the truth of the Mosaic narrative, and those who regard that narrative as a legend would urge that an ignorant and superstitious age sought thus to account for the extraordinary phenomena of the Dead Sea and the district surrounding it.

The narrative of the Jewish captivity in Babylon, again, was formerly a favourite battle-ground in this way ; and in view of the

deciphered cuneiform inscriptions, and other
discoveries of recent years, it is an interesting question whether the Christians or the
scientists displayed the greatest unwisdom in
the controversy.

The fight at this moment wages chiefly
round the Mosaic account of the creation.
Any one who dares even to suspend his
judgment upon the subject is anathematized
by the extreme advocates of faith, and branded
as either knave or fool by the extreme advocates of unfaith.

And yet in fairness it must be admitted
that the charge of intolerance does not apply
equally to both. There is scarcely any religious society in which one need hesitate to
declare his doubts upon this subject ; but a
man must indeed have the courage of his
opinions to own himself a believer in Moses
when among the professors. Intolerance of
this kind savours of persecution, and persecution always secures a temporary success. It

is only the few who ever set themselves to make headway against the prevailing current. If the shout, "Great is Diana of the Ephesians!" be kept up "by the space of two hours," even staid municipal officials will yield to it; and a two hours' *séance* of the professors will silence the doubts of ordinary folk as to the infallible wisdom of science.

Upon any one in whom polemical instincts are strong, the effect is wholly different, and in this particular controversy one is tempted, in sheer wantonness, to take sides with Moses. Poor Moses! If only he had been a real prophet he would have written with the fear of the nineteenth-century scientists before his eyes, and the first chapter of Genesis would have taken the form of an allegory or a poem. Had he written as a heathen philosopher, his cosmogony would now be held up to the admiration of mankind, and his name would be venerated in all the learned societies of the world. But his writings are pressed upon us as being a Divine revelation. Hence the contempt which they excite in the minds of the baser sort of men, who regard everything which savours of religion as a fraud, and the impatience shown, even by men "of light and leading," towards any one who wishes to keep an open mind upon the subject.

But here a sceptic can only criticize, and something more than mere criticism is needed. The subject has such a fascination for many, and such interest for all, that I have availed myself of a friendly pen to state the case from the standpoint of faith. The writer of the following chapter is a sincere, I might say an enthusiastic, believer. He has read in manuscript the chapter now closing, and here is his "apology." It would be easy to take exception to it on many points, but my cordial sympathy with the spirit in which it is written leads me to insert it without note or comment.

CHAPTER VIII.

"I AM a firm believer in the Scriptures, but the attempt to offer a defence of my faith within the limits here assigned to me is a task I decline to enter on. If a personal reference may be pardoned by way of preface, I would say that my faith is not to be accounted for either by want of careful thought or by ignorance of the objections and difficulties which have been urged by scientists and sceptics. But just as the studies which charm the naturalist are an unknown world to those who are ignorant of the book of nature, so also the elements which make the Bible a fascinating volume to the believer do not exist for those who fail to possess the clew to its mysteries. 'Truth brings out the hidden harmony, where unbelief can only with a dull dogmatism deny.'

"Neither can I attempt, under such restrictions, an *apologia* for the Mosaic account of creation. It is a part of the old revelation upon which Christianity is based, and one essential portion of it—the recorded origin of the woman—is enshrined in the Christian system as typical of the spiritual union between Christ and His people.

"But it will not be difficult within a few pages to show grounds for maintaining that the question here raised is still an open one, and that while among scientists generally the cosmogony of Genesis is 'a principal subject of ridicule,' their laughter may not, after all, be the outcome of superior wisdom.

"If I were beginning an octavo volume, I should seek to recapitulate the controversy on this subject, and to define the stage it has at present reached. I should mark the

various positions which have been succes-
sively occupied or abandoned by the disputants, as one or another of the fluctuating
theories of science has gained prominence, or
newly found fossils have added to 'the testimony of the rocks.' But I will content
myself with recalling the main incidents of
the last great tournament upon 'the proem
to Genesis.' The distinguished combatants
were men neither of whom would be selected
as the champion of either side by a properly
constituted 'electoral college,' but a popular
plebiscite would result in an overwhelming
verdict in their favour. I am alluding, of
course, to the discussion between Mr. Gladstone and Professor Huxley in the pages of
the *Nineteenth Century* three years ago.

"In *The Dawn of Creation and Worship*
Mr. Gladstone sought to establish the claims
of the Book of Genesis to be a Divine revelation, by showing that the order of creation
as there recorded has been ' so affirmed in

H

our time by natural science that it may be
taken as a demonstrated conclusion and
established fact.' Mr. Huxley's main assault
upon this position was triumphant. His *main*
assault, I say, because his collateral argu-
ments are not always worthy of him. His
contention, for example, that the creation of
the ' air population ' was contemporaneous
with that of the ' water population ' depends
upon the quibble that both took place upon
the same ' day.'

" Mr. Gladstone proclaimed that science was
perfectly in accord with Moses in recognizing
that life appeared upon our globe in the
order of, first, the water population ; second,
the air population ; and, third, the land population. To which Mr. Huxley replied as
follows :—

" ' It is agreed on all hands that terrestrial
lizards and other reptiles allied to lizards
occur in the Permian strata. It is further
agreed that the Triassic strata were deposited

after these. Moreover, it is well known that, even if certain footprints are to be taken as unquestionable evidence of the existence of birds, they are not known to occur in rocks earlier than the Trias, while indubitable remains of birds are to be met with only much later. Hence it follows that natural science does not " affirm " the statement that birds were made on the fifth day, and "everything that creepeth on the ground" on the sixth, on which Mr. Gladstone rests his order ; for, as is shown by Leviticus, the " Mosaic writer " includes lizards among his "creeping things." '

" The following is the quotation from Leviticus which Mr. Huxley 'commends to Mr. Gladstone's serious attention ' :—

" ' And these are they which are unclean unto you among the creeping things that creep upon the earth ; the weasel, and the mouse, and the great lizard after its kind, and the gecko, and the land-crocodile, and the lizard, and the sand-lizard, and the chameleon.

These are they which are unclean unto you among all that creep' (ch. xi. 29–31, R.V.). And he adds, 'The merest Sunday-school exegesis, therefore, suffices to prove that when the Mosaic writer in Gen. i. 24 speaks of creeping things, he means to include lizards among them.'

"A charming specimen this certainly is of 'the merest Sunday-school exegesis.' The argument which so completely satisfied its author, and silenced his opponent, is nothing but an *ad captandum* appeal to the chance rendering of our English Bible. If the disputants had but referred the question to some more erudite authority than the Sunday-school, they would have discovered that the word translated 'creeping thing' in the eleventh chapter of Leviticus has no affinity whatever with the word so rendered in the twenty-fourth verse of the first chapter of Genesis, whereas it is the identical word which our translators have rendered 'moving

creature' in the twentieth verse, which records
the first appearance of animal life.*

" Mr. Huxley's argument is, therefore, an
overwhelming refutation of his own position.
Science proclaims the seniority of land reptiles in the genesis of life on earth, and
the despised Book of Genesis records that
'creeping things,' which, as Mr. Huxley
insists, must include land reptiles, were the
first 'moving creatures' which the Creator's
fiat called into existence. Will the scientist
now go back upon his argument, or will he
accept the conclusion to which it leads him ?

"For my part, I am willing to make him
a present alike of the conclusion and of the
argument. If Paleontology, instead of con-
firming, as it does, the Mosaic cosmogony,
seemed entirely to discredit it, the fact would
only serve to strengthen the belief I enter-
tain on wholly independent grounds, that the

---

* The word in ver. 26 is *reh'-mes ;* but in ver. 20 it is
sheh'-retz, which occurs ten times in Lev. xi.

fossils are relics of an earlier economy of life, which was engulfed in the catastrophes which produced the present rock-formation of our earth.

"Whether the origin of our globe was nebular or meteoric, it may have been the home of life for ages before the epoch of the Adamic 'creation.' In the record of that creation the conception of a making-out-of-nothing has no place. The Bible is merely the history of the Adamic world, and even that, moreover, only as a background on which to display the great revelation of redemption. The opening verses of Genesis, therefore, mark the successive eras through which the Creator rescued our planet from its 'waste and void' condition,* and prepared

* These same words "waste and void" occur together once again in Scripture. In Jer. iv. 23 they are used to describe the state of ruin to which the Holy Land was brought by the Divine judgments of the captivity era, called "The Desolations." This affords a striking confirmation of the meaning here assigned to them in the second verse of

it as a fitting home for man ; but as to its
origin and earlier history Holy Writ is silent.
'*In the beginning* God *created* the heaven and
the earth.' But when the beginning was, we
cannot even conjecture ; and if we go on to
inquire thc meaning of 'creation,' all that
Scripture will tell us is that 'things which
are seen were not made of things which do
appear'—a statement which will bear every
test that can be applied to it. If in the past
this earth ever suffered a catastrophe such as
that which Scripture declares will engulf it
in the future, the Mosaic narrative would be
at once accounted for and explained.

"I accept that narrative as a Divine revelation ; but the question remains, in what
sense it falls within that category. Was it,
like the prophecies, a communication of
truth wholly beyond the knowledge, and

the Bible. Isaiah xlv. 18 is also noteworthy for the explicit
statement it contains, that, in its original condition, the earth
was *not* " waste."

sometimes beyond the comprehension, of the
recipient? Or was it, like the historical and
didactic books of Scripture, the divinely
controlled and 'edited' record of matters of
which the writers 'had perfect understanding'? Or, as a final alternative, was it the
description of a series of visions accorded
to the seer, to teach the origin and growth of
order and life in our world? It is to this
last hypothesis that I incline. I conjecture
that each era of the work of 'creation' was
the subject of a separate vision. This is the
burden of the first chapter. The second
chapter records a seventh-day vision of the
Creator resting in His work, followed, according to the well-recognized analogy of the
Apocalypse, by a supplementary or interme-
diate vision, giving in fuller detail the crowning event of the creation week.

" But all this is nothing more than a pious
opinion. What faith takes hold of is the fact
that the present economy is the work of a

personal God. I believe in 'the Lord who
made heaven and earth;' who caused 'light
to arise in the darkness,' and chaos to give
place to order; who clothed the earth with
beauty, and filled it with life.

"I mark, too, the method of His handiwork, the order of creation. And here I
accept and endorse Mr. Huxley's *dictum*,
'that it is vain to discuss a supposed coin-
cidence between Genesis and science, unless
we have first settled, on the one hand, what
Genesis says, and, on the other hand, what
science says.' The matter is not ripe for discussion. We are a very long way indeed
from settling 'what science says;' and while
it seems to be taken for granted that 'what
Genesis says' is known to all, closer study
and fuller knowledge will destroy all dogmatism here. When it is said that God
'made the firmament,' and the 'two great
lights,' and the 'beasts of the earth,' the same
word is used as when Noah 'made' the ark,

and Moses the tabernacle. If abiogenesis
were an ascertained fact, and not an exploded
error, the advocate of spontaneous generation
might appeal to the language of the Creator's
fiat, 'Let the waters bring forth,' 'Let the
earth bring forth.' If evolution were an
established truth, the evolutionist might turn
with confidence to Genesis, and mark how
order and life were slowly evolved in the
world. Nor need he find any difficulty in
supposing that mammals may have been
developed among the 'water population,' and
the 'air population' too, before animals of
that order appeared upon the land. Mr.
Huxley's argument on this point is valid only
as destroying the position to which his 'Sunday-school exegesis' forced Mr. Gladstone to
retreat.

"'Evolution is an integration of matter and
concomitant dissipation of motion, during
which the matter passes from an indefinite
incoherent homogeneity to a definite coherent

heterogeneity, and during which the retained motion undergoes a parallel transformation.' If this cacophonous sentence be translated into English, it will be found to contain some undoubted truth, for no error which is not founded upon truth ever takes serious hold upon the human mind. Mr. Spencer does not here pretend, as the careless reader of his philosophy is apt to suppose, that matter itself is capable of producing any such results. Every change is due to motion, and behind motion is the power which causes it. What and where that power is, the scientific teacher cannot tell. He calls it Force, but he might just as well term it Jupiter or Baal. Were he to assert that it is unknown, no one could object, however decidedly they differed from him. But with the aggressive insolence of unbelief he declares it to be 'unknowable,' thus shutting the door for ever against all religion.

"The Christian recognizes the force, and

the effects it has produced, and he refers all to God. He allows a pristine condition of matter described by the philosopher as 'an indefinite incoherent homogeneity;' but as an alternative formula for expressing this, he confidently offers both to the simple and the learned the well-known words, 'The earth was waste and void.' As he goes on to consider the 'integration of matter and concomitant dissipation of motion,' 'And God said' is his method of accounting for the phenomena. The philosopher admits that not even the slightest change can have taken place save as a result of some new impulse imparted by Inscrutable Force. The Christian, in a spirit of still higher philosophy accounts for every change by the intervention of a personal God. It is thus that he explains 'the coherent heterogeneity'—or, to translate these words into the vernacular, the exquisite order and variety of nature.

"But this is a digression. I turn to the

narrative. The earth existed, but it was 'desolate and empty,' a mere waste of waters, wrapped in impenetrable darkness. The changes recorded are, first, the dawn of light, and then the formation of an atmosphere, followed by the retreat of the waters to their ocean bed; then 'the dry land' became clothed with verdure, and sun and moon and stars appeared. The laughter formerly excited by the idea of light apart from the sun has died away with increasing knowledge; and, in our ignorance of the characteristics of that primeval light, it is idle to question the possibility of the third-day vegetation. It may possibly have been the 'rank and luxuriant herbage' of which our coal-beds have been formed; for one statement in the narrative seems strongly to favour the suggestion that our present vegetation dates only from the fifth or sixth day.*

"But this brings up the question, What was

* Gen. ii. 5, R.V.

the creation *day?* No problem connected with the cosmogony has greater interest and importance ; none is beset with greater difficulties. I own to a decided conviction that while the passage clearly indicates our ordinary day, the word is used in a purely symbolic sense. When dealing with a period before man existed to mark the shadow on the dial, and before the sun existed to cast that shadow, it is not easy to appreciate the reason, or indeed the meaning, of such a division of time as our natural day. 'Days and years and seasons' seem plainly to belong to our present solar system, and this is the express teaching of the fourteenth verse.*

"The problem may be stated thus : As man is to God, so his day of four and twenty hours is to the Divine day of creation. And here I would suggest that the 'evening and

* That the earth is older than the sun may at one time have appeared impossible, if not ridiculous. But it seems to be involved in the meteoric hypothesis now rapidly gaining ground with scientists.

morning' do not represent the day, but rather
the interval of cessation from work, which
succeeds and completes the day. The words
are, 'And there was evening, and there was
morning, one day.' The symbolism is maintained throughout. As man's working day
is brought to a close by evening, which ushers
in a period of repose, lasting till morning calls
him back to his daily toil, so the great
Artificer is represented as turning aside from
His work at the end of each 'day' of creation,
and again resuming it when another morning
dawned.

"And is not this entirely in keeping with
the mode in which Scripture speaks of God?
It tells us of His mouth and eyes and nostrils,
His hand and arm. It speaks of His sitting
in the heavens, and bowing Himself to hear
the prayer ascending from the earth. It talks
of His repenting and being angry. And if any
one cavils at this, he may fairly be asked, In
what other language could God speak to men?

"Nor let any one fall back on the common fallacy that a Divine day is a period of a thousand years. With God, we are told, a day is *as* a thousand years, and a thousand years as one day. In a word, the seeming paradox of the transcendental philosophy is endorsed by the express teaching of Scripture, that time is merely a law of human thought. When, therefore, God speaks of working for six days and resting on the seventh, we must understand the words in the same symbolic sense as when He declares that His hand has made all these things.*

"But the mention of the creation sabbath is the crowning proof of the symbolic character of the creation 'day.' God 'rested on the seventh day from all the work which He had made.' Are we, then, to suppose that He resumed the work when four and twenty hours had passed? Here, at least, revelation and science are at one: the creation sabbath

* Isa. lxvi. 2.

has continued during all the ages of historic time. *God* is active in His universe, *pace* the atheist and the infidel, but the CREATOR rests. Scripture, indeed, tells of a supreme catastrophe that is yet to engulf our planet, and of a new creation which is to follow it, of which the resurrection of Christ is the earnest and pledge. But these are topics I must not enter upon, for I wish to keep in touch even with those who differ from me. I content myself with noticing the well-recognized fact that the creation sabbath is a vast period of time, and urging that the working days of creation must be estimated on the same system.

" This must be borne in mind as we proceed. The 'water population' and the 'air population' belong to the same 'day;' but ages of time may have intervened before the appearance of the latter.* So also with the 'land

* Of course the suggestion of the Authorised Version is erroneous that the water was the birthplace of the " feathered

I

population' of the sixth day. For aught
that we can tell, the appearance of man may
have been separated from that of other mammals by a period of time as prolonged as
that which divides the present hour from the
close of the creation 'week.' *

"But all this is mere conjecture. And my
object in suggesting it is not to frame a
system of interpretation, but to enter a *caveat*
against confounding the teaching of Scripture
with any system of interpretation whatever.
I deprecate the idea that I am posing as a
'reconciler.' I have no such ambitious aim
as that of seeking to convince the scientists.

tribe." The words are, "Let the waters bring forth abun-
dantly the moving creature that hath life, and let fowl fly
above the earth in the open firmament of heaven."

* The second chapter indicates that there was an interval
between the formation of the man and of the woman. The
Paleontologists' proofs that earth was the dwelling-place of
intelligent beings at a much earlier period are not complete
enough to justify any definite comparison between those
earlier inhabitants and the Adamic race. Indeed, it is
doubtful whether they afford certainty of being pre-Adamic
at all, though the probabilities are strong in that direction.

I wish rather to warn the faithful against assaults upon the Mosaic cosmogony, based on 'the merest Sunday-school exegesis' on the one hand, and on the *theories* of science on the other. The *facts* of science in no way clash with Scripture. They serve only to assist us in understanding it aright.

"Of the origin of our world the first chapter of Genesis tells us nothing, save that 'in the beginning,' whenever that was, God 'created' it. It may be, as Mr. Tyndall says in his Belfast address, that 'for æons embracing untold millions of years, this earth has been the theatre of life and death.' But as to this the 'Mosaic narrative' is silent. It deals merely with the renewing and refurnishing of our planet as a home for man. And this, moreover, as I have already urged, to prepare the foundation for the supreme revelation of redemption. Let the authority of Scripture be undermined, and the whole fabric of the Christian system is destroyed.

But in these easy-going days the majority of 'those who profess and call themselves Christians,' being wholly destitute of the enthusiasm of faith, are helpless when confronted by the dogmatism of unbelief. It is a day of opinions, not of faith, and widespread apostasy is the natural result. But Christianity is eternal, because it is Divine."

CHAPTER IX.

"THE rational attitude of a thinking mind towards the supernatural is that of scepticism."* Scepticism, remember; not agnosticism. "Agnosticism" is Greek for ignorance, and ignorance is disgraceful. We doubt, not because we wish to refuse knowledge, but because we crave certainty. In this sphere more than any other, we desire to guard against being imposed upon. What is presented to us as religion is for the most part a fraud. In this domain, no less than in the world of science, we are confronted at every step with some phase or other of our old friend "the confidence trick." If only we

* Mill's *Essays on Religion.*

will but accept as certain truth the unproved theories of the geologist, the facts he lays before us will commit us to his account of the origin and history of the habitable earth. If we will but adopt the unproved hypotheses of the evolutionist, he will betray us into the admission that man "came originally from stocks or stones, from nebulous gas or solar fire." So, again, if we will but commit ourselves to the mystic power of the priest, he will secure for us mental peace and spiritual benefits in this world, and endless happiness in the next. Or, turning to the half-faith Christians, they too will promise the highest good, both here and hereafter, if only we will consent to make our home in the splendid edifice which they have built upon a quicksand.

These words are not the expression of a prejudice, nor are they framed in any spirit of hostility to Christianity. Neither are they intended to furnish an excuse for going back upon the conclusions already accepted. The path of the truth-seeker is beset with discouragements and difficulties, but to reach such a goal no amount of patient effort can be excessive. There is a God, and man is His creature. Religion, therefore, is a reality, and the existence of a revelation is *a priori* probable. But what is the true religion? And where is the revelation to be found? The "thinking mind" is sceptical, not from love of doubting, but from love of truth. Is it matter of wonder that men should refuse the guidance of those whose faith is inseparably identified with superstition, or of others whose belief, if indeed they believe at all, has no reasonable foundation whatsoever?

And it is a grievous calamity that so many to whom we might naturally look for light— accepted leaders in the world of science— have become so blinded by prejudice against religion, that common men are led to assume that between superstition and infidelity there is no middle standing-ground. And yet their own example might teach a far different lesson. At what cost of sustained and disciplined labour, often baffled, sometimes entirely fruitless, have they deciphered the mysteries of the book of nature! If, even in the natural world, truth must needs be sought after as for hidden treasure, how much more in the sphere of the supernatural?

And whatever judgment may ultimately be passed upon Christianity by the matured ntellect of the race, we may rest assured that it deserves far more consideration than these men accord to it. Even if its transcendental claims be rejected, even if it be denied the unquestioning submission which, regarded as a Divine revelation, it demands, it still stands out as the noblest conception of natural religion which the mind of man has ever formulated. "Christ is still left, a unique figure, not more unlike His predecessors than all His followers, even those who had the direct benefit of His personal teaching."

It is to that life that even John Stuart Mill thus appeals as furnishing "a standard of excellence and a model for imitation" which "can never more be lost to humanity." "Who among His disciples," he asks, " or among their proselytes, was capable of inventing the sayings ascribed to Jesus, or of imagining the life and character revealed in the Gospels ? Certainly not the fishermen of Galilee ; as certainly not St. Paul, whose character and idiosyncrasies were of a totally different sort ; still less the early Christian writers, in whom nothing is more evident than that the good which was in them was all derived, as they always professed that it was derived, from a higher source."

Do not such words as these suggest the thought that if only Christianity would forego its transcendental claims, if it would but consent to make terms with unbelief, we might

seize upon that matchless life as "a standard
of excellence and a model for imitation," and
realising that, in all its unique perfections, it
is no mere poet's dream, but a great living
fact in history, we might seek to trace the
footprints thus left to guide us, as we set out
upon the path of "patient continuance in
well-doing," which finds its sure reward in
"honour and immortality"?

But the suggested compromise Christianity
refuses. That it should fairly represent the
teaching of thousands of Protestant pulpits
only proves that men are as dishonest in
religion as they are in trade. What can
possibly be gained by participating in such
a fraud? Once we reject the claim of the
Bible to be "the oracles of God," then, as the
writer of the preceding chapter has justly
urged, Christianity is destroyed. The life of
the Nazarene still remains, as the imperish-
able possession of humanity, but the transcendental facts and mystic doctrines which

are the foundation and essence of the Christian system must be at once and for ever abandoned. The miraculous birth, resurrection, and ascension, the presence of Christ in heaven now, and His future return to judgment, are one and all but myths which every fearless thinker will reject, and with them the whole cluster of Christian doctrines based on them. All faith is at an end, and even scepticism is deprived of its rational foundation ; for doubt implies an insufficiency of evidence, and of valid evidence here there is absolutely none. We are thus brought face to face with blank agnosticism, after all.

The most sincere of doubters surely may be pardoned if he start back at sight of such a goal. The jaunty and superficial scepticism of the day can claim but a distant kinship with the earnest doubts of men who recognize the gravity of a crisis, which, as has been justly said, "no one but a fanatic of materialism can see without the most

serious misgiving." *   Some such thoughts as
these must have inspired that articulate sigh
in the poetry of Matthew Arnold—words of
exquisite sadness and beauty—

> "The sea of Faith
> Was once, too, at the full, and round earth's shore
> Lay like the folds of a bright girdle furl'd ;
> But now I only hear
> Its melancholy, long, withdrawing roar."

And what if Christianity be true ?   Is it so
clear a case that the faith of apostles and
martyrs was a mere delusion—the faith
which, even in its most corrupted forms, inspired the scholarship and chivalry of medieval
Europe, and which in brighter and happier
times has been inseparably identified with
all that is noblest and best in human effort
and progress ?

It is impossible, surely, for any one who
has ever "loved the Bible," † and felt the

---

* Professor Goldwin Smith.

† "I loved the Bible, and was prompted by that love to
commit large portions of it to memory."—*Fragments of
Science*, i. 383.

glow of high and holy thoughts which it
begets, to mark without misgivings the inevitable goal to which popular Christianity
is hurrying. And when such thoughts
even now arise within the mind, leading the
memory back to earlier, it may be happier
and better days, scepticism itself seems sometimes to turn traitor, and, taking sides with
faith, to bid the doubter doubt the wisdom of
his unbelief. Is this but an unwholesome
mist, begotten of discarded superstitions?
or can it be the lingering halo of departed
truth?

Are we really prepared to hold "that
Christianity is not so much as a subject of
inquiry"? Is it "now at length discovered
to be fictitious"? Is it "so clear a case that
there is nothing in it"? What if, after all,
Christianity be true? Can it be, as some
would tell us, that, amid the din of discordant
philosophies and rival creeds, the listening
ear may catch the echoes of a Divine voice

which scatters doubt and brings confidence and gladness to mankind?

All such misgivings are foreign to the spirit of much that passes for philosophy to-day, but the genuine truth-lover will honestly avow them. Their influence upon the minds of men is strikingly displayed in the position now occupied by the majority of religious teachers. With enthusiasm which is well feigned if it be not sincere, they cling to the superstructure of Christianity, although they have utterly discredited the foundations upon which it rests. But with the free thinker no such compromise is possible; and as he stands at the parting of the ways, and marks the abyss to which the wide and well-worn road of unbelief inevitably leads, he cannot fail to glance back upon the path of faith, now almost deserted, and to wish that the old beliefs were true.

THE END.

For EU product safety concerns, contact us at Calle de José Abascal, 56–1°,
28003 Madrid, Spain or eugpsr@cambridge.org.